The San Damiano Cross
An Icon of the Crucifixion

Madeleine Stewart

Conard Press, 27 Coney Island, BT307UQ, Northern Ireland.

Conard Press

27 Coney Island
Co Down
BT307UQ
Northern Ireland.

Website: conardicons.com

ISBN 978-1-9161432-0-3

Images with the assistance of:
www. kieranbroganphotography.com

Printed in Northern Ireland by Kaizen Print, Belfast
Cover design by Niamh Cassidy, Kaizen Print.

COMMENTS

I have waited for this book since I first began bringing pilgrims to Assisi 35 years ago. While everyone who writes about the San Damiano Crucifix acknowledges it to be an icon, this is the first explanation that concentrates on its profound iconic meaning, a welcome addition to all the literature that surrounds this symbol of Franciscan identity and solidarity.
André Cirino, OFM—Franciscan Pilgrimage Programs

I found Madeleine's booklet to be one of the best 'explanations' of the San Damiano Crucifix that I have read so far. I highly recommend this book to all lovers of icons but especially to those who have fallen in love with the very particular icon known as the San Damiano Cross.
Jesus Mary Pawley, OFM. Conv.

This beautiful new study of the famous Franciscan icon draws on Madeleine's deep knowledge of iconography, along with her heart of faith, to provide rich new insights. It is a gift to the Franciscan family, and to everyone who wants to deepen their faith in the crucified and risen Lord.
Helen Julian, CSF. – (presently serving as Minister General of the Anglican Franciscans)

THE AUTHOR

Madeleine Stewart, a member of the Association of Iconographers of Ireland and of The British Association of Iconographers, has been painting icons for twenty years. With an engaging love and enthusiasm for her topic, she gives talks, workshops and retreats, introducing participants to the basic principles of Iconography in the Byzantine tradition.

She has worked as an Architect and Town Planner, is a published Children's Author and a tutor in Creative Writing. This booklet is her first non-fiction work and her first entry into the world of self-publishing.

ACKNOWLEDGEMENTS

My sister, Paula Pearce OFS, is responsible for arousing my interest in the San Damiano Cross. She has been a source of encouragement and inspiration throughout. Through her, I have met a number of Franciscans, many of whom have become friends through their involvement with the emerging manuscript. I am privileged to have had such benevolent support.

I am grateful to everyone who provided feedback on earlier drafts of this booklet. The comments I had were very helpful, constructive, and, most of all, encouraging. They have contributed a great deal to this project.

When I started writing, I lacked the computer skills necessary to create a coherent document. I could not have produced this booklet without the unfailing patience and generosity of my son, Nick Maxwell and his lovely wife, Sophie. I am still learning and I apologise for any evident lack of professionalism.

I was not, and still am not, adept at manipulating images. My photographer friend Kieran Brogan sorted every problem with skill and tireless commitment.

I am grateful to Willa King for enthusiastic interest and for proofreading the penultimate draft.

I am fortunate to have the support of The Association of Iconographers of Ireland, in particular Dick Sinclair, Collette Clarke and our Maestra, Eva Vlavianos. Eva has taught us the technique of icon painting and most importantly, has nurtured an understanding of the theology and language of this sacred art. Dick has been a constant source of information and insightful advice.

My friend, Bruce Clark, has consistently supported me with his gentle encouragement and sound guidance. He has helped me to appreciate something of the great riches of the Orthodox Church and facilitated my journey towards a better understanding of Orthodox spirituality.

PREFACE

There are such deep riches in the Orthodox tradition of Iconography that this booklet can only skim the surface, however some insight into this sacred art is essential in order to appreciate the visual imagery of the San Damiano Cross; for the San Damiano Cross is a great icon. A crucifix hanging over the altar in a Catholic church is an essential feature of the Western, Latin, tradition. To have an Eastern icon in this role affirms it as a symbol of unity between the Eastern Orthodox Church and Western Catholicism: whilst being an icon, true to the Byzantine tradition, it is also a crucifix, suitable to be hung above the altar in a Catholic church

Individual icons of the crucifixion in the Eastern Orthodox Church were generally rectangular in shape. The use of a panel shaped like a cross is a Western influence, another way in which this particular icon brings the traditions of East and West together.

Later medieval painted crosses gradually became more westernised; the figure of Jesus became more 'solid' and the simple frame disappeared.

An understanding of the San Damiano Cross as an icon may promote greater interest in the spirituality of the Orthodox Church and the wonderful gift it brings in the sacred art of iconography.

Christ prayed for His followers to be one. In 1995 Pope John Paul II wrote a pastoral letter, *Orientale Lumen,* in which he stated that 'The first need of Catholics is to be familiar with the ancient tradition (of the Eastern Church) and to be nourished by it.' He longed for the Church 'to breathe again with both lungs.' Bringing the two traditions together as it does, The San Damiano Cross can be seen as a bridge to better understanding and reconciliation; a fundamental aim of Franciscan spirituality.

In the icon of San Damiano there is a call to see victory in suffering. St Francis wrote his joyful *Canticle of Creatures* when he was suffering terribly in his body. The great Franciscan saint, Padre Pio, spoke of the tremendous spiritual value of consecrated suffering.

The Eastern tradition focuses on Christ's victory - the West on His suffering. Both aspects of the cross are uniquely inherent in the cross of San Damiano; Christ the Victor in the visual theology of the icon, and the suffering of Christ as central to Franciscan spirituality.

It is my hope that this booklet will contribute towards a richer appreciation of the beautiful and unique icon known as the San Damiano Cross and to a better understanding between West and East.

In memory of my beloved son Andy
and
for the Abbot, monks and staff at Douai Abbey
who supported me both physically and spiritually during
the last months of Andy's life.

The SAN DAMIANO CROSS - An ICON of the CRUCIFIXION

THE STORY BEGINS

I was not enthusiastic at all when my sister asked me to give a talk on The San Damiano Cross to a group of secular Franciscans on pilgrimage to Assisi.

'But, Paula,' I said, 'I don't know anything about it!'

She replied with great confidence.

'You know so much about icons, you are bound to have some insights which would be helpful to us.'

I was not convinced that I would have any 'insights', but I did agree to give the talk, thinking that I would have time to read a few booklets beforehand.

And, for me, that is where a very special relationship began.

The next day the group was scheduled to visit San Damiano.

SAN DAMIANO

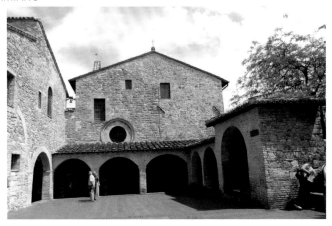

San Damiano is a small cluster of stone buildings, central to which is the little church dedicated to San Damiano. A short distance outside Assisi, it nestles into the hillside, set amongst olive and cypress groves.

It is a place of great peace, far from any urban froth, granting panoramic views over the countryside below.

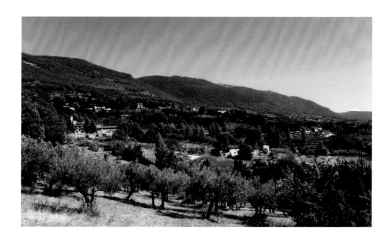

In the time of Francis, the little church was in ruins. Within the ruins, an icon of the crucifixion hung above the altar space. The year was 1206. Francis, passing by, was drawn to enter the church. Inside he beheld the icon and he opened his heart before it. The San Damiano Cross is a large icon, and in that tiny chapel, it would have had a tremendously powerful presence. Francis would have been close to it, close to the eyes of Jesus, as he prayed:

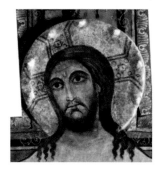

'Most High and Glorious God,
enlighten the darkness of my heart.
Give me sincere faith, confident hope, perfect
charity, profound humility, comprehension and
discernment
that I might understand your holy and true
command.'

God replied. Francis heard a voice speak to him from the icon:
'Francis, go repair my house, which, as you see, is falling into ruin.'
God's word to Francis was intimate, using his Christian name, the name used familiarly by his parents and friends. There is here a sense of Francis being anointed by God, chosen for his work. As God spoke to Francis through the icon of the crucifixion at San Damiano, God not only confirmed Francis as His servant, He confirmed the validity of the sacred icon as a channel of access to the divine.

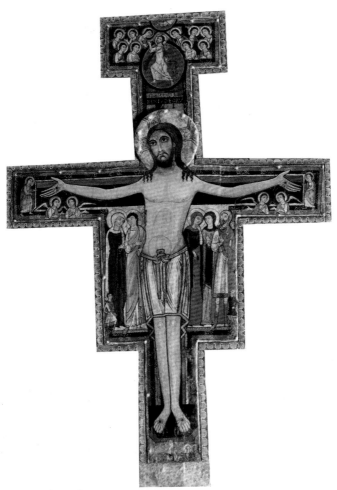

The San Damiano Cross.

The experience affected Francis profoundly and changed the direction of his life. His life as a dedicated servant to God began.

Later, San Damiano became the first convent occupied by St. Clare and her sister nuns. There, the sisters worshipped and tended the sick; keeping the vow of poverty and leading simple, chaste lives. The original San Damiano Cross which hung in the chapel, was cared for and venerated by the nuns until, after the death of St Clare, they moved to Assisi in 1253. A replica now hangs in its place, above the altar in the chapel of San Damiano. The original cross hangs in Santa Chiara in Assisi.

The convent at San Damiano has been retained in its original state and is partly open to pilgrims. It is cared for by the Friars Minor. The Sanctuary of San Damiano is a very special place. Much of the convent of St Clare is as it was when she lived there; the refectory with its simple wooden tables and benches, St Clare's Oratory (where the Blessed Sacrament was kept) and the sisters' dormitory where St Clare died. These are open for pilgrims to visit. There is no charge. It is a place of prayer and contemplation, not a museum.

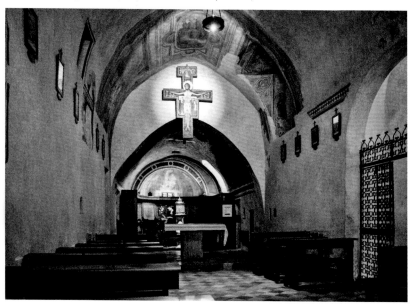

The visit to San Damiano was deeply moving. Seeing where St Francis prayed before the cross, being able to kneel in that same church below a replica of the same cross brought me into the mystery of the cross and the spirituality of St. Francis and St Clare. For the first time, I paid full attention to the San Damiano Cross.

Looking more objectively at the icon, I noticed that there was something very odd about the base of the cross.

We returned to Assisi; to Casa Papa Giovanni, where the group was staying. In the shop at the Casa I found two booklets about the San Damiano Cross. After supper, I took the booklets upstairs to the library and settled down to read them in preparation for my talk.

BOOKLETS

On reading through my recent purchases, I felt that the perceptions of the authors, emanating from the Latin culture of Western Catholicism, were rooted in knowledge of the written Word. In their devotion to the cross they make links and share spiritual insights which are an excellent aid to prayer. However, some of their observations indicated a lack of familiarity of the 'rules' of Eastern iconography. To be fair, very few western commentators, even art historians, recognise the sophisticated symbolism and theological integrity which is inherent in classic Byzantine iconography.

In terms of religious imagery, the difference between Western and Eastern culture is immense. I found many instances in both booklets where the imagery had been interpreted without the benefit of a knowledge of the very particular 'language' of iconography. To give an example; M Picard reflects on the face of Jesus being 'veiled'. The face of Jesus would never be intentionally veiled in an icon. Icons show the theological truth. They do so with clarity. The idea that Jesus would not be fully present to his people is contrary to the theological truth and would never be communicated in iconography. That is not to say that Jesus' face does not look darker today: it does!

I realised that my own background in iconography did indeed enable me to share insights into the icon which were not easily recognised by Western commentators. Perhaps Paula had been right after all.

The next day I went to Santa Chiara where I would see the original icon.

SANTA CHIARA

Having read the booklets, I was keen to look specifically at the face of Jesus and at the foot of the cross to see if I could gain more insight as to why the former was dark and the latter so unfinished looking.

On entering St George's chapel in Santa Chiara, I felt a little disappointed that the cross was hung so high. With my arthritis, it was uncomfortable to look up. Because of the discomfort, I found it hard to pray with as I would have liked.

Kneeling in St George's Chapel in Santa Chiara, in front of the icon, I prayed. I did not want any study of the cross to take precedence over focusing on it in prayer. I didn't appreciate then how this study would bring me closer and closer to God and the loving Heart of Jesus.

However, I did have a talk to prepare for and it was time to make a start!

The San Damiano Cross in Santa Chiara

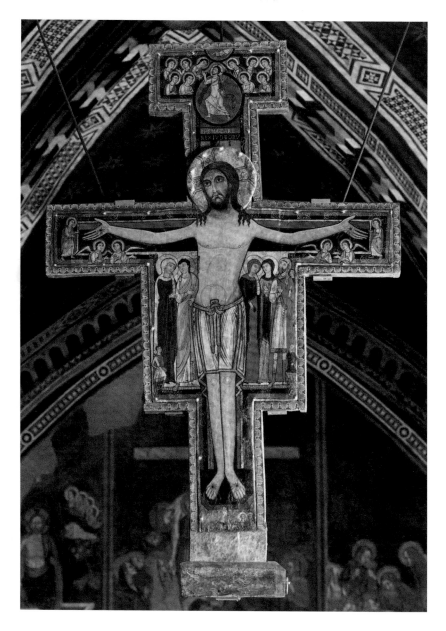

Looking at some technicalities:

Firstly, I was again struck by the anomaly of the base of the cross.

My knowledge of 'rules' of iconography gave me the confidence to be certain that the marble tile at the base of the cross would not have been an original feature. Just above the marble tile, I could see that there was considerable deterioration of the painting. I considered it likely that the tile was a repair of some kind.

Secondly, I was able to see that the cross is not completely flat. The face and halo of Jesus are painted unto a wedge shape. This, roughly circular, section of the cross is leaning out and down. I realised that this could be the reason the face of Jesus is darkened. The outward angle meant that this part of the cross was more susceptible to the effects of rising smoke, incense, and other vapours, which may have affected it over time.

(see side view of the top of cross illustrated)

All that apart, I was profoundly moved by the icon, which is a most exceptional image of The Crucified Lord.

The beauty of the love, humility and gentleness in the face of Jesus calls you into communion with Him.

The icon is beautifully constructed to show the theology of the crucifixion and to be a visual translation of the gospels.

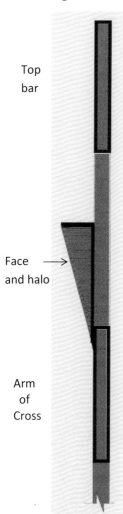

Top bar

Face and halo →

Arm of Cross

Elevation of top of the cross.
Straight on view from RHS

On my way back to Casa Papa Giovanni, I stopped at the wonderful stationery shop, *Pietro Vignati,* just off the square in Via Portica. I was going to need a flip chart, some tracing paper and a ruler. I had some homework to do before my presentation to the group the next evening.

HOMEWORK IN THE CASA

I started with the foot of the cross. Looking carefully at my copy of the cross, I could see that the shell border was rudely interrupted where the tile had been attached. The border is an integral part of an icon. It defines a 'window' into the spiritual world. Originally the border would, most assuredly, have surrounded the whole of the icon.

I could see where studs had been used to secure the inner border of gold. Using simple symmetry, it was apparent that the lowest set of studs was missing.

I found a book on Italian religious art in the library. It had pictures of a number of painted medieval crosses. Several of these showed severe damage to the foot of the cross. My deduction that the stone tile was a 'repair' gained credibility – it seems that damage affecting the base only, or most severely, was not an uncommon feature to be found on medieval painted crosses.

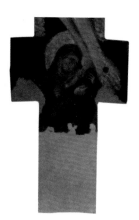 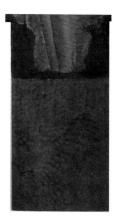 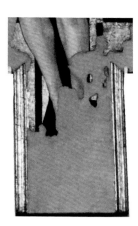

Now certain that the tile was indeed a repair and that the original cross had been longer, I started with the studs. As previously observed; the gold element to the border of the San Damiano Cross had been secured using studs. Using symmetry, and my ruler, I could estimate the position of the 'missing' studs. This enabled me to establish a good approximation as to how much longer the original cross would have been.

I now had enough information to propose that there would have been six full length figures at the foot of the cross.

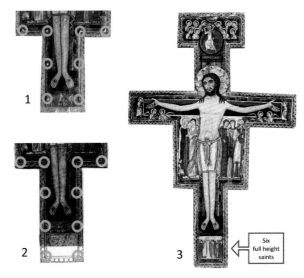

I used my recent purchases to highlight the positions of the studs in the gold strip border (1) and then to indicate the probable position of the 'missing' studs and the resulting position of the original border. (2) Using symmetry and the sizes of the heads visible, I was then able to indicate how the original cross would have been long enough to accommodate a panel of six full height saints. (3)

(I provide a full, illustrated explanation of these findings on pgs. 41-56)

At the time, I did not attempt to identify these saints. That would come later.

There are many aspects to the language and symbolism of iconography which aid correct interpretation of the icon. I spent time looking at the image and all its features. Fundamentally, as an icon of the Crucifixion, it presents the truth of our redemption and draws us into The Infinite Love. It expresses our redemption, through the sacrificial death of Jesus, who submitted, with such love, to the will of The Father. *'And for us men and for our salvation, He came down from heaven, and was made man.'*[1]

I studied the icon with increasing interest and with full attention. My understanding of the language of iconography did, to my own surprise, enable me to see things which might not otherwise have been apparent.

I was ready to give my talk.

---

[1] Nicene-Constantinople Creed 381

It seemed to me essential, as a preface, to convey something of the essence of iconography even though this is a 'backdrop', found in, but not specific to, the San Damiano Cross. I began with a brief overview of Medieval Imagery and The Sacred Art of Iconography.

MEDIEVAL RELIGIOUS IMAGERY

Many of you are already familiar with the significance of The San Damiano Cross within Franciscan spirituality. Through its powerful imagery, it has an inherent role as an inspiration to prayer and meditation.

The San Damiano Cross is also of special interest as an icon, for icons are rich in meaning, rooted uncompromisingly in biblical truths and church dogma. A deeper understanding of the theology behind its artistry will enhance our appreciation of its roots and symbolism, draw us closer to the spirituality which inspired it, and open our hearts to the sacred truths it portrays.

The use of art works in religious life goes back to the earliest days of the Christian faith. A simple drawing of a fish was used in the catacombs. This was a symbol of Christian belief derived from the Greek word for a fish: IXΘΥΣ or IXΘYC. 'Jesus Christ' is IHCOYC XPICTOC in Greek. The symbol of the fish was used because the letters of the word gave the initials of Jesus' name and title. (IX: Jesus Christ, Θ: Theou/God's, Y: Yios/Son, Σ: Σoter/Saviour) In iconography the first and last letters of the name Jesus Christ, IC XC, are used as an abbreviation of His name and are usually found close to His halo.

By early medieval times, church art had developed as holy people and biblical scenes were portrayed in mosaics and frescos and as individual 'pictures' on boards.

There was a consistency of style very close to that of classic Byzantine orthodox iconography. This is exemplified by the frescos on the walls of the ancient crypt recently uncovered below the Duomo in Sienna. They are alive with icons of saints and biblical scenes which conform perfectly in style and content to the guiding principles of Orthodox iconography. Constantine Cavarnos, in his *'Guide to Byzantine Iconography'* describes how the highly stylized art of iconography derived from a fusion of elements taken from *'classical Greek art and from the Hellenistic art of Egypt, as well as from other traditions, particularly that of Syria.'*

However, as the Western, Latin Church and the Eastern, Orthodox Church grew apart, so also did their artistic interpretation of religious subjects.

In the west, religious art evolved in union with the artistic mores of the secular world. It moved towards 'realism'; solid body forms set in dramatic locations, time and place confirmed by the use of shadow and perspective, emotions powerfully portrayed. These directions were exalted to artistic heights in the Italian Renaissance. Art in the Western Church has continued to 'move with the times', reflecting artistic styles prevailing in secular society.

In complete contrast, the Eastern Orthodox Church retained the use of stylized figures, developed from the use of a symbolic language of iconography rooted in a strict compliance with theology. Iconography would retain its own integrity down the ages, unmoved by secular artistic developments. Compare Leonardo da Vinci's Italian Renaissance painting of St John the Baptist with an icon of the same saint. (known as St John The Precursor in the Orthodox Tradition). The contrast is stark. The icon is not naturalistic; the figure is stylized. St John is thin, reflecting his penitential life. Leonardo's John is very much 'of the flesh'.

St John the Baptist, Leonardo da Vinci

Icon of St John the Precursor

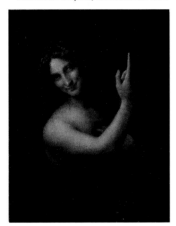

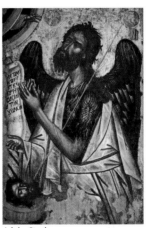

Paris, Louvre © Photo SCALA, Florence

Adobe Stock

Icons, and particularly an early and complex icon, like the San Damiano Cross, can look strange, and even, unattractive, to the Western eye. Eyes used to the realism, in a material sense, of Western renaissance art, and in modern times, to the highly individual works by artists regarded as great, can easily fail recognize the beauty of icons; rarely do they see the integrity of the theological truths which they portray.

This study of the San Damiano Cross is based on a degree of knowledge of iconography. It is intended to facilitate a better understanding, and hence open the way to a greater love of this most remarkable icon. An introduction to the principles of iconography is a necessary starting point to such understanding.

THE SACRED ART OF ICONOGRAPHY

During a period of iconoclasm, the Eastern Imperial Court forbade the use of icons. This provoked treatises in defence of icons. The role of icons was scrutinized and debated. The result was, in the end, to set icons within a strict doctrinal and theological context. The 4th Council of Constantinople (869-870) linked the approval of icons to the clarification of the true nature of Christ as being fully human and fully divine. What was made flesh, visible to human eyes, could be represented by material means. Thus, Christ could be shown in an image, but not God the Father. (other than as He is shown in Christ-*He who sees me, sees the Father.*) There were strict codes of practice as to how sacred images were to be 'written'.

Icons were to show theological truths, not an artist's individual idea as to how someone or somewhere might have appeared. The Eastern Church retained the concept of icons as being set out of time, space and other attributes which defined the subject in a temporal context. In keeping with the strict codes relating to the theology and symbolism of icons, they are commonly described as being 'written' rather than painted and 'read' rather than looked at.

As spiritual truths are timeless, so is the perspective used in iconography. The comparative size and/or position of figures illustrate a spiritual relationship, not a temporal one. Thus in classic Byzantine iconography you would never see the Holy Family portrayed with Joseph as the central dominant figure, Joseph being the lesser saint in theological terms would not be dominant in either size or position; such 'icons' of the Holy Family are invariably Western in origin, painted in the style of icons, but lacking their theological integrity.

The written words on sacred themes in the Latin Church were, for a time, scrutinized by the church authorities and, if appropriate, given an 'imprimatur' to indicate that the content was in keeping with Church doctrine. In a similar way, in the Eastern Church, particular icons were approved as being theologically correct. Only these approved prototypes were to be copied. The

Orthodox Church brings a great gift to the Christian world in the consistency with which the language of icons has been preserved from the earliest days of the Church.

A classic icon of the Eastern Church will have no shadows as these are indicative of a specific time. They will not use perspective, which defines a single viewpoint in a temporal location. There will be no subtle and expressive portrayal of the skin or of the solid weight of the body. Instead the human form is stylized and elongated, not naturalistic. This stylization emphasises the 'other worldliness' of the subject.

Each holy figure is portrayed with his or her, own identifiable set of features; St John the Forerunner is always shown with stylized wild hair, the hair of the Mother of God is concealed beneath a veil and mantle. Jesus' hair is neatly groomed, wavy with a centre parting. St Peter has short, thick wavy grey hair and a thick, short, wavy grey beard. St Paul is partially bald, with a little tuft of hair on top of his head. He has a beard; long and thin, often hanging in tendrils.

Jesus is usually shown wearing a red tunic *(chiton)* and a blue cloak *(himation)*; the red indicating his divinity and the blue the humanity which He took on.[2] Gold lines on his garments signify his divinity. The Risen or Transfigured Christ will be robed in white. As an infant, Jesus is shown with adult proportions, indicating that, even as a child, he had the wisdom of God; spiritual maturity.

The name of a saint will be written on an icon of that saint. The names may be shortened but would be familiar and easily recognised; IC XC = Jesus Christ.

Gold was used to portray the uncreated light of God; the divine light of heaven. Saints in iconography are shown as being within this domain rather than earth bound. A gold background is therefore a common setting for a saintly figure. Halos, shown as a circular disk around the head, denote that the person endowed with this feature is within the light of God. In iconography, all saints will be shown with a halo. Jesus alone has vertical and horizontal lines marked in the halo around His head. These lines symbolise His cross and remind us that He gave *'His life for the ransom of many.'* (Mt 20:28). Greek letters often

[2] Terzopoulos, Rev Dr Costantine translator, *What Do You Know About Icons?* An Aesthetic, Historical and Theological Approach to the Icons of the Orthodox Church in the form of Questions and Answers. Pub by Holy Monastery of Saint John the Baptist, Kareas. 2001, ISBN 960-8447-07-0 (pg. 82)

found within the cross are O, ω, and N. These letters are an abbreviation of 'The Being' and are generally translated as meaning 'He Who is.' They are derived from God responding to Moses' question as to who He (God) was. 'I am who am.' (Ex 3:14)

As saints were depicted as being in the spiritual world, earthly emotions or situations were not dominant features; if a saint had been martyred, that saint would be shown carrying a simple cross. This symbol tells us the theological truth of their having died a martyr's death, not the manner of their death. Icons of the crucifixion do not show emotion reflecting the intensity of Christ's physical pain. They show the theological truth of Christ's loving submission to His Father's holy will. They show His love for mankind. They show His victory over death and sin. They show our redemption; a theological truth rather than an event in time.

Holy people are almost always depicted with full or three-quarter faces. Figures with their heads in profile are generally specifically not holy. Look at icons where Judas is present and you will notice how his face, alone amongst the apostles, is in profile. This is the general rule, although in specific icons a face in profile is used to emphasis the direction of interest, for example the face of St Thomas is often in profile as he faces the wounds in the resurrected Christ.

All the senses of the saint are shown in an icon. They are alert, aware of all our spiritual needs and of the presence of God. They are fully attentive to God and fully attentive to us.

Saints' eyes will be wide open, inviting the viewer into prayer and meditation. Eyes are large. They are the windows of the soul. Just as eye contact is critically important in human communication, so the eyes of the saints portrayed in icons are important; their expression drawing us into relationship. At least one ear will be clearly visible, indicating that the saint is attentively listening, both to our prayers and to the Word of God. Mouths are closed, serene and wise, never gross or sensual; never smiling, as that would indicate a fleeting emotion rather than the eternity of heaven. The nose, elongated as a sign of saintly dignity, is always visible. Hands are shown, indicating the sense of touch. They are elongated, reflecting the 'other worldliness' of the saint depicted.

The position of the hands will be significant. A hand might be raised in blessing, holding a book (The Word of God) or in some other way contributing to the interpretation of the icon. A hand which is holding something holy will often be wholly or partially covered. Figures are typically full height or from head (and halo) to below the waist, so that the hands are visible

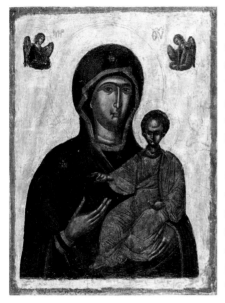

In icons known as Hodegetria, 'She who shows the way,' the Mother of God is pointing to the child she carries. This gesture is read as saying *'This is the Way, the truth and the light.'* Her other hand is partially covered, denoting that what she is holding is sacred.

Within the Byzantine tradition, Mary is always known as 'The Mother of God', defining her true theological status. The gold stars on her garment symbolise her virginity. The deep red of her garment, the colour worn by Byzantine royalty, defines her as 'Queen'.

Consistent geometric relationships are another feature of iconography. The basic unit of measurement is – THE NOSE!

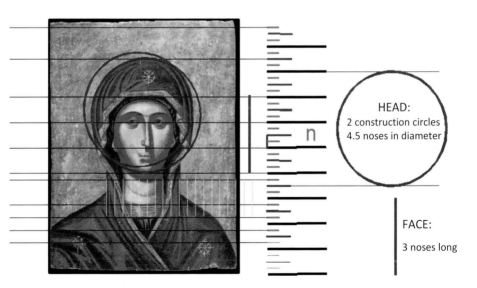

HEAD:
2 construction circles
4.5 noses in diameter

FACE:
3 noses long

Note how key features of the image relate to multiples of 'n' (length of nose).

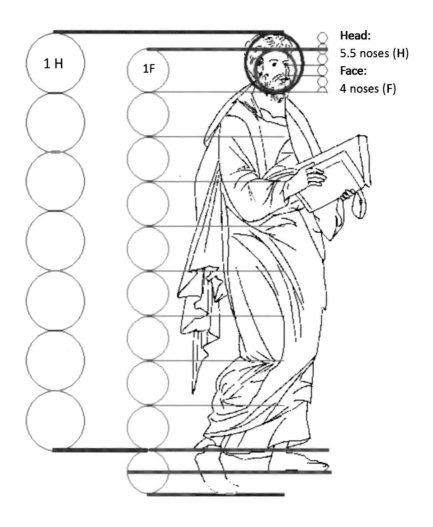

Head:
5.5 noses (H)
Face:
4 noses (F)

1 H

1F

The illustration above is based on an icon of St Matthew in the National Museum in Ohrid

The proportion of full height of a figure in relation to the length of the face or head may vary, but will be consistent within any particular location and era. ***The Painter's Manual of Dionysius of Fourna*** [3] teaches that *'in the whole figure of a man there are nine faces, that is to say nine measures from the forehead to the soles of the feet.'*

[3] Heatherington, Paul translator, *The 'Painter's Manual' of Dionysius of Fourna*. Pub by The Sagittarius Press, USA. 1974, ISBN 0-9503163-0-X.

Geometric relationships underpin the drawing of the San Damiano Cross. In this instance the heights of the figures in the icon are 8.5 times the heights of the heads.

Icons were framed, often through the use of a painted border. The frame emphasises that we are drawn through this window to another world; the spiritual world. We are in communion with God through contemplation of His Word portrayed visually. The frame should not detract from, nor overshadow, the content. A red colour was traditionally used as a framing border to recall the blood of the martyrs of the early church.

Quite apart from the differences in artistic style, there was also a difference in the attitude of the renaissance artists of the west to that of eastern iconographers. The former were creative artists, not always renowned for living virtuous lives. There is a belief that Carravaggio used his mistress as a model for the Mother of God. This would have been considered by Orthodox believers as being sacrilegious; scandalously lacking in reverence and respect.

The iconographers of the east were holy monks, praying and fasting as they worked. Iconography was part of a monastic way of life, just as the creation of beautifully illustrated manuscripts of prayers and scripture were part of medieval monastic life in the west.

The fact that icons convey theological truth is fundamental to understanding the imagery.

There is much more to be said about the symbolism and theology of icons; volumes. A list of books etc. for further reading can be found at the back of this booklet. However, I hope that I have told enough to give some insight into this sacred tradition and prepared my readers to look at the icon of the cross of San Damiano in more detail.

Having introduced something of the language of iconography, I shared my insights into the imagery of the icon with the pilgrim group.

I had used the tracing paper and a ruler to work out and then present my findings regarding the original length of the cross.

PRIMARY FEATURES OF THE SAN DAMIANO CROSS

The scallop shell border and the inner border of gold, provide a frame through which we are taken to the spiritual realm.

The use of contrasting bands of red and black remind us of our redemption from death to life.

Jesus' face, eyes open, expressing loving submission to His Father's will.
The halo around His head confirms His being in the uncreated Light of God.

Angels

Blood issues forth from the wound in Jesus' side

Witnesses to the Crucifixion below Jesus' right arm.

Mary, His Mother
St John, the Beloved Disciple
Longinus, the Roman soldier who pierced Jesus' side with his lance

Jesus' garment symbolises His Royal Priesthood

THE FOOT OF THE CROSS
As explained in the text, the stone inset tile at the base of the cross is a 'repair'.

The centre left saint was an archangel, most probably St Gabriel. The two saints on the left side of the panel cannot be identified for certain but there is a possibility that they were St John the Baptist and St Simeon.

The Arc of Heaven

Angels within the heavenly realm

Jesus enters heaven, victorious over sin and death

Inscription: 'Jesus (IHS) of Nazareth, King of the Jews.' (in Latin)

The arms of Jesus, are open and giving. Blood spurts from His wounded hands

Angels

Witnesses to the Crucifixion below the left arm of Jesus:

The Crowd
Mary Magdalene
Mary, the Mother of James
Roman Centurion
Stephaton (Individual who gave Jesus a sponge soaked in vinegar)

THE FOOT OF THE CROSS
Originally there would have been six full height saints in a panel at the foot of the cross.

St Cosmas

St Stephen

St Damien

St Gabriel
or possibly St Michael

There is a full explanation as to who the saints in the panel at the foot of the cross were and how long the original cross was, in the body of the text. (*pgs 41-55*)

READING THE ICON; WHAT WE SEE IN THE SAN DAMIANO CROSS

The icon is framed by a painted border of scallop shells, and within this, by a gold band. The base of the cross has been damaged and the continuity of the border broken.

Originally the base of the cross would have been longer; the frame would have been continuous and the panel within, below Jesus' feet, would have shown six full height saints. I was able to show the pilgrim group drawings on my flip chart to illustrate this point. (*upgraded illustrations on pgs 44-48*)

Today there is a marble tile fixed to the damaged portion at the base of the cross. There are only two heads of the original six saints visible today. They are looking up at Jesus.

The subject of the icon, the crucifixion of Jesus, is powerfully portrayed as Christ's victory over death and sin: his gaining our redemption through His infinite love for His Father and for mankind. The subject is the Crucifixion, portraying the theology of love over sin, life over death. The icon is knit through with this contrast; black symbolising death and division from God, red symbolising life in God, redemption through the blood of Christ. In appropriate contexts, red is also symbolic of the Holy Spirit. An inner border of red alongside black is dressed over with a series of delicate white vines.

The figure of Jesus, and especially His holy face, is dominant in this icon.

The figure of Jesus, His face so full of serenity, is not overwhelmed by anguish and suffering. His arms stretch out along the arms of the cross, not hanging, but reaching; hands open and offering. His body is shown erect and still upon the cross. He is freely giving all, for love of us and in obedience to the Father. The icon shows the eternal theology of the crucifixion, not the torture of the moment.

The vertical section of the cross below the arms is widened and in this central panel, witnesses to His crucifixion are portrayed.

At the top of the cross, Jesus is blessed by God in the arc of heaven and the angelic host welcome the victor home.

JESUS, THE CRUCIFIED LORD

The figure of Jesus dominates the icon. It is nearly three times larger than the figures below his outstretched arms. His golden halo extending over the shell frame almost to the edges of the panel, gives great visual emphasis to the face of Jesus encircled within. The gold has dulled over time. Just imagine how dominant the halo and the head of Jesus would have been when the gold shone brightly; candle light reflections shimmering with life.

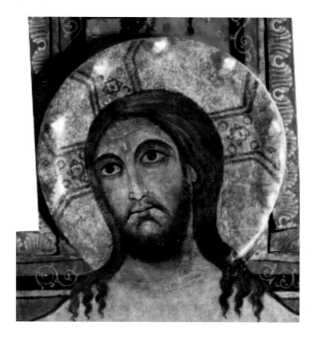

The holy face is the central focus of the icon, and, within the face; the eyes. Jesus' eyes are lifted, looking into the distance, not in a way which excludes us, but so wide, open and compassionate as to draw us also into the spiritual world. They are not the eyes of a victim in human torment. They are serene and full of love.

They express His loving, humble obedience to the Father and his compassionate love for all His children. Here is the fulfilment of God's plan for our redemption. Here is victory over sin and darkness. This is the truth this icon tells and all else portrayed confirms this truth.

The figure of Christ stands erect, not hanging, on the cross. His head is not bent in defeat; it is raised, serene and sorrowful, in loving communion the Father. The saviour's arms are outstretched, wide and embracing, his hands open and offering. All of humanity is encompassed within his arm reach. His offering of himself to the Father is complete in dignity and full in love. The nails through Christ's hands and feet and the wound in his side are shown as fountain heads from which His blood is flowing to restore humankind to grace; His open hands giving to us freely and welcoming us to new life.

Jesus' hair is shown as neatly groomed. Torture and death do not overwhelm His dignity. The features and beard of the Christ figure are consistent with how the holy face is portrayed in icons. The way his hair falls in thin ringlets is symbolic of it being wet due to sweat and blood. The face is full. Jesus is always available to us. All the senses are expressed. Notice how Jesus' ear is shown and not hidden by His hair. This emphasises the fullness of communication we are offered, Jesus listens to us. Jesus is wholly attentive to the word of God.

Jesus' throat is shown as being strong and wide. It is the channel through which the life of the Holy Spirit breaths. His body is elongated and stylized. Simple lines indicate His bodily form. There have been suggestions that the Holy Spirit can be seen, in the form of a dove, on Jesus' forehead. This is fanciful and has no basis in fact. Icons are explicit. Equally fanciful is the notion that the head of God the Father is shown in profile in the lines on Jesus' torso. Firstly, as previously noted, icons are explicit. Every feature of relevance is clear and meaningful. Secondly, only people considered unholy are shown in profile.

It has been observed that the head and throat of Jesus appear to be darker than his body. This is not because they were originally painted darker, or 'veiled'. It is for some technical reason related to aging, a possible reason being that this portion of the icon, including the halo, is set proud and tilted forward. It was therefore more susceptible to darkening over time due to the smoke rising from candles and incense.

JESUS' HALO

The gold halo around the head symbolizes the brilliance of divine light in the person who lives in the intimacy of God. A halo is painted around the heads of holy people recognised as being saints, living in the divine light of God. In this icon Jesus' halo is the most dominant single feature of the icon. It stretches the full width of the cross, extending over the scallop shell border. It is an elliptical shape, having a width of $7n$ and a height of $6.5n$. ('n' = the length of Jesus' nose). Within this elliptical disc, the face of Jesus inclines to His right. The shape ensures balance as the visual weight of the wider portion of golden halo counter balances the visual draw to the opposite side created by the inclined head of Jesus. It also allows the halo to extend the width of the cross, establishing a strong, stable, central focus.

Within the halo, the cross markings refer to the crucifixion and identify the figure as that of Christ. The decoration within the three sections of this cross are based on squares and sets of four, a reference to the four corners of the earth; the whole world. Jesus laid down His life for all. Circles and diamonds call to mind Christ's eternal nature.

The halo, and the face and throat of Jesus within the ellipse are on a wedge-shaped base, so that the top of the halo is some inches proud of the cross behind. Thus, Jesus' face and halo are physically tilted down towards us, beautifully expressing His love for us.

THE ARMS OF THE CROSS

There are full figure angels, one on each extremity of the arms of the cross. They look and point inwards to Jesus. Their wings are not shown, but their neatly curled hair with ribbons clearly identifies them as angels. Two pairs of angels with open wings are shown beneath the upraised wrists of Jesus. These angels point to Jesus and, looking at each other, share in the communion of love. Visually these angels bring harmony and enclosure to this window into the sacred. Visual harmony and balance are qualities found in all good icons.

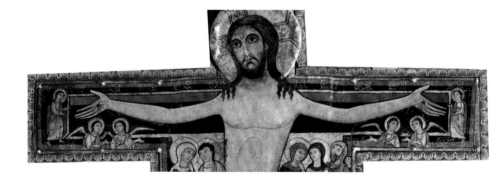

Their encircling of Jesus reminds us that all the angels in heaven were focussed on the person of Christ, their God.

The angels are in total unity with God. They are also close to man, ever working to bring us closer to God. They look to Jesus, aware of our redemption from sin through His death on the cross.

ARMS and HANDS

Jesus' arms reach out wide and giving. His hands are open and offering. The shape of His hands nestles within parallel arcs of circles. The attitude of loving, willing, humble obedience is unmistakable

The nail wounds in His hands spurt blood. The blood of Jesus is very powerfully portrayed. It flows down His arms and falls on the witnesses below.

JESUS' GARMENT

The cloth around His waist is neat, not ragged. In spiritual terms, nothing of Christ could be ragged. Icons show theological, not earthly, truths.

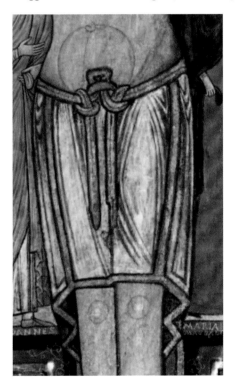

The gold border to the cloth is symbolic of the divinity of Christ. The thrice looped knot is a reference to the Trinity.

The garment is meaningfully evocative of the priestly undergarment of the Old Testament (Ex 28:2) signifying the priesthood of Christ and his self-sacrifice on the cross.

THE FEET OF JESUS

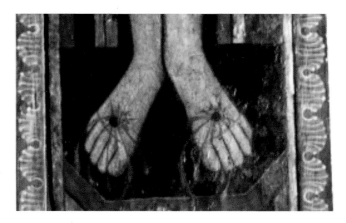

The weight of dark black around the feet of Jesus, from which His body rises, affirms his resurrection from the tomb and our redemption from sin through the cross.

The blood spurting from the wounds in Jesus feet is painted with great life and power. The vitality of the blood of Jesus and its redeeming power flows in abundance.

The red border below Jesus' feet defines the bottom of the panel showing the crucifixion.

The damaged panel below this red border will be considered later.

FROM DEATH TO LIFE

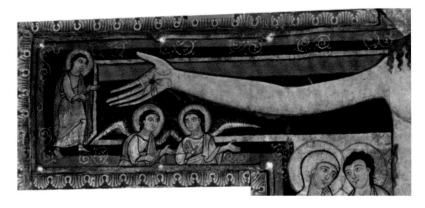

In iconography the colour red, in some contexts, is indicative of the Holy Spirit. It is also associated with life. Black is most usually associated with sin and spiritual death. The striking contrast between red and black, evident as a background theme of this icon, reminds us that, through the death of Jesus on the cross, we are brought from death to life.

Notice how the nails through Jesus' hands are positioned exactly where a black horizontal band gives way to a horizontal band of red above. His blood has brought us from sin and death into the light, restored our relationship with God. In this icon there is no depiction of a material, wooden cross, there is instead the theology of the crucifixion, the transformation of humanity's relationship to God: black to red, death to life, redemption through the sacrificial love of our God.

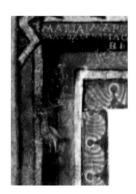

A series of delicate white scrolls decorate red and black framing borders within the gold border. These are a reference to the vine and to the tree of life.

On the right-hand side of the cross, below the figure of Mary Magdalene, a rooster has been painted. Significantly, it bridges across the black inner bordering at this point. The rooster announces a new dawn. It is a symbol of our redemption through the passion and death of Christ.

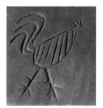

I recently noticed the same symbol on an Irish Penal Cross.

It may also recall Peter's betrayal and the lessons in forgiveness and humility which ensued.

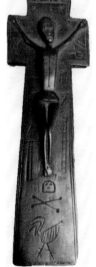

THOSE PRESENT AT THE CRUCIFIXION

Witnesses to the crucifixion are shown below the outstretched arms of Jesus on the widened central panel of the cross. There are five main witnesses, two lesser witnesses and another minor witness.

PRIMARY WITNESSES

On the right side of Jesus are his Holy Mother and St John. On His left are Mary Magdalene, Mary, the mother of James, and the Centurion. Their names are written in Latin below.

HALOS

The three Marys and John, the beloved disciple, have halos, signifying that they are saints. The centurion does not have this status.

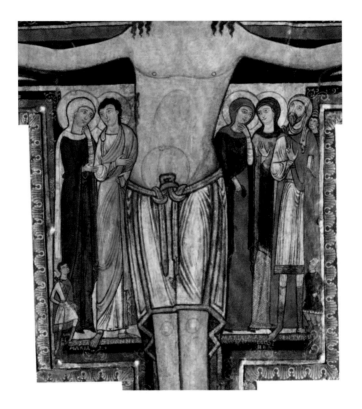

There is a slight difference of size in the halos. The halo of the Mother of God being the largest, that of St. John is the next largest, then that of Mary Magdalene, which is slightly larger than that of Mary the mother of James. The relative size of their halos reflects their relative status in theological terms.

HANDS

Mary, the Mother of God and Mary Magdalene hold hands to their faces, a sign of grief. Mary, the mother of James holds her hand up in dismay. The Mother of God and St John both point towards Jesus with their right hands signifying 'This is the way, the Truth and the Life,' keeping our focus on Jesus. St John holds a tuck of his mantle in his left hand. This gesture speaks of sorrow and loss. Mary Magdalene does the same with her right hand.

The centurion's right hand is raised, facing forward with his two smaller fingers folded, his thumb open and his first two fingers raised together. This hand gesture means that he is *speaking with authority*, a reference to his pronouncing the great truth: *'Truly, this man was the Son of God.'* (Mk 39:15)

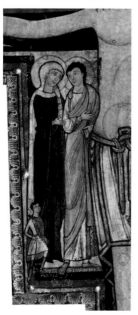

The importance of this essential truth is reinforced by his holding a writing tablet or scroll in his left hand. His hand is covered, which means that what he is holding is sacred. This tells us that the tablet is 'The Word of God', announcing the truth of Christ's divinity. Inspired by the Holy Spirit, the centurion was announcing the word of God. In bringing the centurion's revelation to our attention, the icon is explicit in pronouncing the truth; Jesus Christ is the Son of God.

STANCE

The two saints on Jesus' right, The Mother of God and Saint John, are inclined towards each other; heads almost touching, halos overlapping. Their right hands are in line, making a strong visual link, acting almost as an arrow pointing us to Jesus. The figures are not separated; there is a powerful sense of closeness between the two. Neither saint is looking up at Jesus although Mary's head is inclined also towards her Son.

The figure of John melds into Jesus' waist and hips. The curve of John's upper arm is a continuum of the curve of Jesus' waist.

The drape of John's mantle sits perfectly into the line of Jesus' garment alongside. The hem of John's mantle is on the same line as that of Jesus' garment. The folds in the upper part of John's mantle echo the arc of Jesus waist, resulting in a close visual bond between the two saints and the figure of Jesus. There is here close intimacy and harmony.

In addition to the symbolic meaning, the detail of John's left hand holding a tuck in his garment is designed to arrest any visual movement away from Jesus. The tuck breaks the line of the hand and takes the eye back to Jesus.

The two holy figures are intimately bound together and intimately bound to Jesus. Looking at this expression of deepest love, we cannot but be moved, reminded that Jesus, though in agony, gave us Mary as our Mother also.

The two Marys on Jesus' left side demonstrate similar closeness.

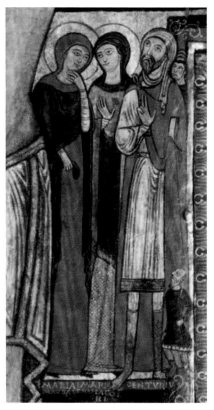

In its portrayal of the saints below Jesus' arms the icon presents us with a communion of love; a unity of faith. Contemplation of the saint witnesses as individuals would be rooted in our knowledge of them gained through scripture and other holy sources.

The remaining primary witness, the centurion, stands proud of Mary, the mother of James. His figure is not melded together with those of the saints. He alone, amongst the primary witnesses, is looking up at Jesus. The others, the saints, are so close to Him in their hearts that they are 'with' Him, not outsiders looking 'at' Him. They suffer themselves, feeling for His suffering in their hearts, rather than 'watch' Him suffer. They love Him.

COLOURS

The five main witnesses are stood against a gold background. The gold represents the uncreated light of God, the heavenly domain.

The colours of the garments worn by The Mother of God and St. John are significant in iconography. The reddish purple of Mary's cloak is taken from the colour associated with the Empress in the Eastern Imperial Court and affirms her as Queen of Heaven. It also signifies that she took on divinity when she conceived Jesus. The blue dress below signifies her human dignity, spiritually enlightened and imbued with wisdom through the power of the Holy Spirit. Her white veil signifies her purity. Generally in the Eastern Church the virginity of the Mother of God is represented by gold stars on her mantle. This icon though, is early and is Syrian in style. Similarly, St John's white tunic attests to his purity. The pink of his outer garment is the colour of a youth.

The colours of the Romans' (the Centurion and Longinus) uniforms are the colours which Roman soldiers wore. They therefore aid recognition.

Mary Magdalene is traditionally shown wearing bright red in icons, so again the colour aids recognition. Her mantle is usually deep blue, as it is in this icon. There are no colours specific to Mary the mother of James. The deep blue of her mantle is the same colour as Mary Magdalene's cloak and the dress of the Mother of God. This makes a visual link between the three women. The light viridian green of her dress, which is only visible from knee height down, is found in the angels' mantles.

There are decorative patterns on two garments; the veil of the Mother of God and the dress of Mary the Mother of James. The veil enfolds the head of the Mother of God and drapes down over her right shoulder. Decoration adds status to the wearer. The Mother of God and the mother of James are relatives and this status is acknowledged in the decoration of their garments. Mary, the Mother of God's decorated garment is around her head, reflecting a higher status than that of the mother of James.

As with every aspect of iconography, the aim is to show spiritual and not earthly realism. The decoration on the garments is clear and beautifully executed but there is no attempt to show the folds in the garment interrupting the pattern. The imagery is purposefully not naturalistic but is stylized and symbolic.

(The decorative trims to the garments of Longinus and the Centurion are symbolic of their earthly, not theological, status.)

LESSER WITNESSES

LONGINUS and STEPHATON

There are two smaller figures, known witnesses to the crucifixion, in this central portion of the icon. In the lower left-hand corner, to the right of Jesus, is the small figure of Longinus. Longinus is the Roman soldier who pierced Jesus' side with his lance. Tradition holds that he became a Christian.

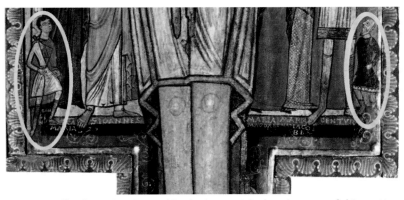

A smaller figure is mirrored in the lower right-hand corner of this section of the icon. This figure is Stephaton, the name given to the person who held a sponge soaked in vinegar up to Jesus' mouth.

On the San Damiano Cross both these figures look up at the face of Jesus, while Longinus' face is shown to us, that of Stephaton is not. It is in profile, indicating that he is not holy. Longinus is named, whereas Stephaton is not. Longinus is below, even touching, the most holy Mother of God, whilst the

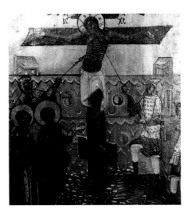

smaller figure of Stephaton is on the left and below the Centurion, a far lesser person in theological terms. Thus, although the two figures mirror each other, there are clear indications that Longinus is favoured, whereas Stephaton is not.

The inclusion of both Longinus and Stephaton as minor characters at the crucifixion is found in several prototypes of icons of the crucifixion. As in the illustration opposite, Stephaton is always shown on Jesus' left and Longinus on His right.

BEHIND THE CENTURION

Outside the gold background, there is a small head visible behind the Centurion's shoulder. There have been some suggestions as to who this person might be. Some have proposed that it is the Centurion's son, another that it is in fact the artist, yet another that he is a temple guard. Rather than rely on our imagination as to who this might be, in iconography we look at the facts. Firstly, he is a witness to the crucifixion. Icons are clear in their portrayal of truths as found in the biblical references. This panel contains witnesses, it is not going to show a person who was not identified as a witness in scripture.

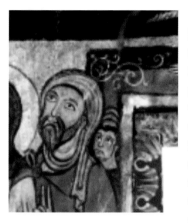

Like the other lesser witnesses, he is looking at Jesus. When painters of icons, influenced by Western artistic movements, have put themselves into one of their paintings, they have tended to show themselves as looking directly out at the viewer. Further, it is most likely that the iconographer was a monk. There is no support whatsoever of the 'self portrait of the artist' theory. Indeed, such vanities, though not unknown in western renaissance religious paintings, are definitely not part of the eastern tradition.

The title of 'Centurion' refers to an officer in the Roman Army who had charge over 100 men. The Centurion whose son was cured was from Capernaum, a village on the west of the Sea of Galilee over 100k north of Jerusalem. The Centurion in Jerusalem, given the task of overseeing the crucifixion, will not have been the same Centurion as the one from Capernaum whose son was cured. The suggestion that the small figure behind the centurion's shoulder is the son who was cured is thus far from credible. There is no possible reason to believe that a soldier father would have brought his child to watch a crucifixion.

The suggestion is fundamentally disproved by the fact that the panel contains the witnesses to the crucifixion identified in the gospels. Icons portray only theological truths, not artists' imaginative ideas.

Finally, the small head is not that of a child. In iconography, size relates to theological status or to a design element of the icon, not to size in a worldly sense. The figure has a clearly drawn beard and moustache. It is the head of an adult man.

Above his head are three even tiers. The tiers are face coloured and echo the shapes of the tops of heads. This face, and the hidden faces behind it portray 'the people' described in St Luke's gospel; *'The people stood by, watching'*. (LK 23:5) The relatively small size of the face, or faces, indicate that, in theological terms, they are relatively unimportant.

THE UPPER PART OF THE CROSS

THE INSCRIPTION

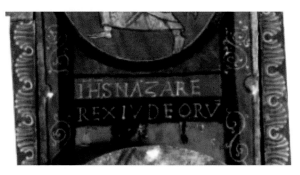

Above the figure of Christ, a bold black horizontal band is surmounted by a bold red band. On these, 'Jesus of Nazareth, King of the Jews' is written. The abbreviation '**IHS**' for the name of Jesus comes from the first three letters of His name in Greek. The remainder of the inscription is in Latin. Scripture tells us that Pilate instructed a notice, so worded, to be attached to the cross of Jesus. It also serves as the written name of the figure in accordance with iconographic practice and it identifies the cross, again in accordance with the biblical text.

JESUS LIVES

A roundel is set into the cross above this inscription. The lower half of the roundel sits in the top of the vertical section of the cross. The upper half is within the widened top section where the angelic host is shown, thus, it joins heaven and earth. The roundel has a narrow outer frame of black, then an inner ring of gold and inside this ring the roundel is red. The colours symbolise the fact that the light has overcome the darkness of sin and death.

Within this roundel is the figure of Christ.

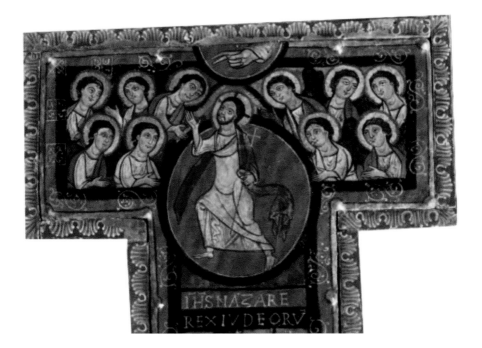

The figure of Jesus is in swift movement heavenwards. His head and right hand are shown reaching upwards out of the roundel; through its boundaries.

The faces of the closest four angels are set along the upper arcs of the roundel. Christ has accomplished his mission, redeemed us from the power of sin. He returns to The Father. All heaven rejoices.

In his left hand, Christ carries a cross, the symbol of martyrdom. In iconography, holding a simple cross signifies that the saint was a martyr. The cross held by Jesus is unique in that it is golden and mounted on a staff. It is both a martyr's cross and a symbol of kingship.

A dark red priest's stole (epitachelion) swings over His left shoulder and is bunched around His left hand, confirming His priesthood. His garment is white, as it is in icons of the Transfiguration and of the Resurrection. The top of the halo of the victorious Christ is just below the 'Arc of Heaven.'

THE ARC OF HEAVEN

The Arc of Heaven is shown as a semicircle, symbolising that the unseen part of the circle exists as heaven which *'eye hath not seen.'*

Within the Arc of Heaven, a hand is shown in blessing. The hand is Jesus' hand, because Jesus, and not God the Father, may be shown (because Jesus took material form on earth whereas God the Father did not). However, in this context, Jesus' hand is taken to represent the Hand of God the Father. *'He who sees me, sees the Father.'*

THE ANGELIC HOST

The angelic host is represented by ten angels; a top row of three and a lower tier of two, to each side of Christ's rising figure. Three angels on each side are shown with welcoming hands outstretched towards Jesus, worshipping Him and hailing His victory. The two outer angels in the top tiers turn towards each other, emphasising the communion of love in heaven and echoing the attitudes of the saints at the cross.

Angels are shown with wings, signifying their role as messengers and with halos, signifying their heavenly abode. They are always shown with ribbons in their tidy curled hair, a sign of order and compliance with God's holy will. The outward reaching ends of the ribbons symbolise the angel's reaching out to us, drawing us to God.

FRAME

The San Damiano Cross has a simple painted border framing around the edge of the cross. In the symbolism of iconography this establishes the icon as a window to the sacred. The frame is simple in its muted harmonious colours, the background colour being a dull red onto which a repetitive pattern of scallop shells is painted. The continuous linked pattern indicates the eternal nature of the icon's message. The choice of shell reflects an association with heavenly beauty, inspired by the shimmering mother of pearl internal glaze, and of eternity, perhaps on account of its circular shape and the fact that scallop shells, being flattish, endured the weathering of the sea better than most shells. The scallop shell is the badge of a pilgrim, still used today by pilgrims on the Camino of Santiago di Compostello. Another link to the gospel is that scallop shells were used as water scoops in baptism.

Within the subtle shell frame is an inner framing of gold. It is likely that the shell and gold border would have encompassed the whole of the icon in its original form. It is unthinkable that an icon would have been painted with the border being cut through, as it appears today at the base of the cross.

The base of the cross deserves a detailed inspection because there are several indications that the original cross was longer than it is as we see it today.

THE BASE OF THE CROSS

1. The shell border is rudely interrupted. This is obviously not a feature of an original icon. The whole work has been constructed and executed in a most diligent and consistent manner. The cutting through mid-shell, as now found above the tile inset at the right-hand side, is out of keeping with the rest of the image and inconsistent with the nature of icons.

The frame, setting the icon and its spiritual domain apart from the world, is an important feature of any icon. The frame to the original icon would have been complete. The shell border, the gold border and the black and white painted inner border would have encompassed the image, establishing a window into the sacred.

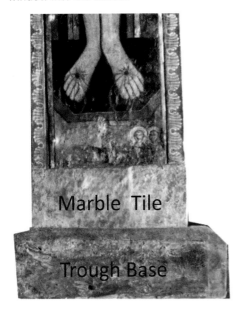

Marble Tile

Trough Base

2. An inset tile is not found on any other icon. It will not have been part of the original icon.

3. The top parts of the saints discernible are shorter than the regular proportions found in icons. Further, rows of saints are nearly always full height.

4. Icons are constructed on geometric relationships. The proportions, content and detail at the foot of the cross in the icon, as it is presented today, lack the orthodoxy found in iconography.

DAMAGE AT THE BASE OF THE CROSS

Severe and disproportionate damage being found at the base of early medieval crosses is not unusual.

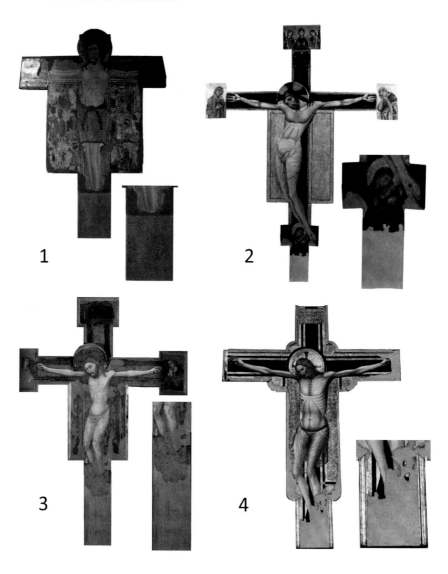

The examples above show such damage.

1. Croce dipinta Inizio del Duecento, Siena Pinacoteca Nationale.

2. Croce dipinta Chiesa di Sant' Angelo al Cassero Pinacoteca.

3. Francesco di Segna, Crucifix, 1328-39, Buonaconvento
   Museo d'Arte Sacre della Val d'Arbia.

4. Giovanni Rimini, Crucifix, 14th Cent.

Other examples of crosses exhibiting similar deterioration of the base are:

- The Crucifix from the Chiesa della Grazie at Montecerboli, which is in excellent condition-except for the base on which no trace of painting remains.
- The Crucifix from San Pietro in Villore San Giovanni d'Asso, now in the Sienna Pinacoteca Nationale, which is badly damaged throughout, but most severely at the base.
- The Crucifix di Santa Chiara now in the Museo Civico in San Gimignano on which nothing of the original paintwork remains below Jesus' ankles.
- The Crucifix painted by Alberto Sotio, 1187, now in the Duomo in Spoleto. This cross bears some similarity to the San Damiano cross.
- Croce dipinta, Assisi, Basilica inferior di S. Francesco.

The San Damiano Cross must have suffered similar damage. The decision to 'repair' it with a marble tile may have been to facilitate it being touched in veneration by pilgrims.

The investigation to deduce something about how the cross originally looked began with tracing paper and a ruler in the library of our hostel, Casa Papa Giovanni. I continued the study at home with the aim of providing an indicative image as to how the cross would have looked when St Francis prayed before it and God spoke from it.

Having worked as an architect for many years, I had the advantage of having an excellent technical drawing programme on my computer. This enabled me to measure distances, copy, draw accurate circles etc.

Icons are ideal subjects for such scrutiny, based as they are on geometric relationships. I was able to build in the length of Jesus' nose as a unit of measurement, and that led to the discovery of the extent to which this dimension is intrinsic to the design of the image.

My first task was to make an evaluation as to the length of the original cross.

THE LENGTH OF THE CROSS

How much longer was the original icon? Looking at the gold frame inside the shell border on the San Damiano cross, a number of raised studs are clearly visible. These are ringed in white on the illustration.

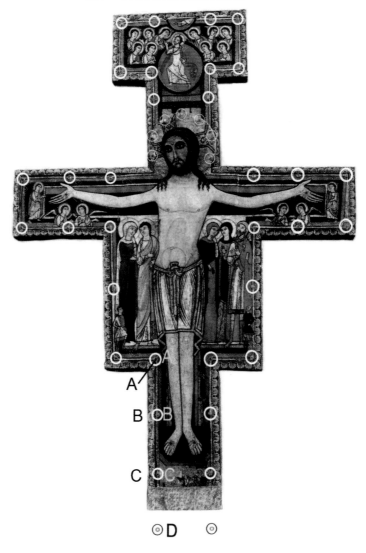

From the position of these studs it is evident that the lowest corner studs are missing. Using simple symmetry (AB=CD) a likely position for the missing studs at D can be established.

Using the deduced position of the missing studs we can add the likely extension of the shell border.

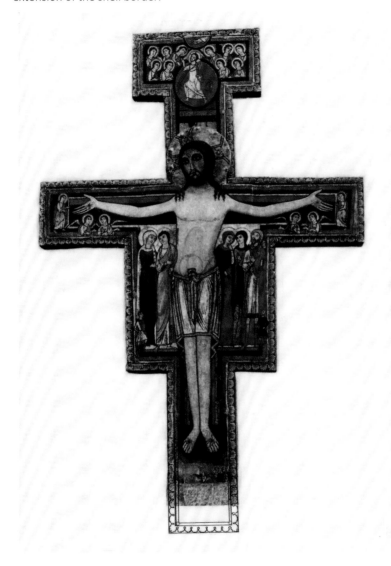

Thus, we now have a probable length of the original cross.

The validity of this deduction is confirmed by another set of symmetrical forms. It gives an equal dimension above and below the black element of the icon around the feet of Jesus. Such symmetry is a feature of iconography.

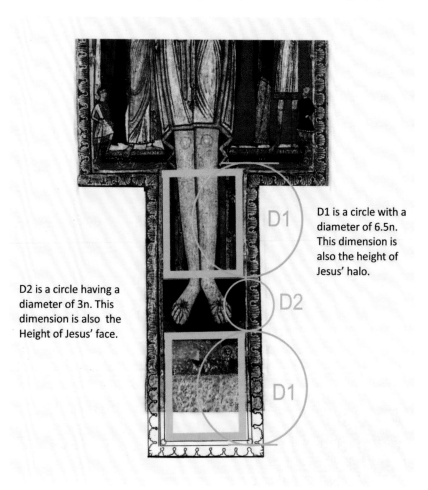

D1 is a circle with a diameter of 6.5n. This dimension is also the height of Jesus' halo.

D2 is a circle having a diameter of 3n. This dimension is also the Height of Jesus' face.

Further, the depth of these panels is equal to the depth of Jesus' halo. The depth of the panel in between corresponds to the length of Jesus' face.

Next investigation: what was painted on the original cross in the panel below the feet of Jesus?

The full height figures below the arms of Jesus are elongated in the customary fashion. They are eight and a half times the length of the head.

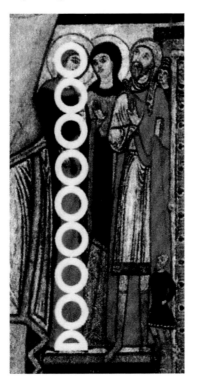

This gives us the geometric proportion for the figures used in this icon.

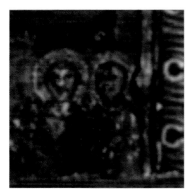

All figures will have this same proportion of head to full body height, irrespective of whether the figures are big or small.

Happily, we have two clear(ish) heads of saints in the lower panel, certainly enough to get a dimension for the height of a head and thus, by applying a multiplication factor of 8.5, we can deduce the heights of the full figures.

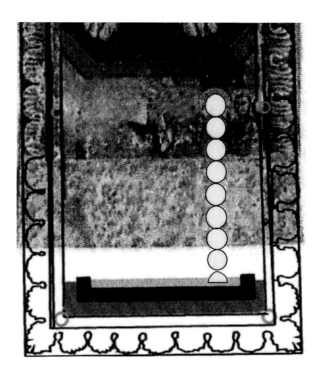

As illustrated above, this dimension fits perfectly with an original length of the cross identified through positioning the missing studs.

Width-wise it can be stated with confidence that there would have been six saints side by side in the panel at the base of the original cross: the two central saints would have been a little larger than the other four.

At this point we have established a probable length of the original cross and that the lowest panel would have portrayed six full height saints.

The next stage in the study is to establish who these saints were.

For this investigation I relied totally on my knowledge of the language of iconography. This sacred language is consistent with regard to the symbols and features used to aid identification of particular saints.

We have some clues to work on.

SAINTS AT THE FOOT OF THE CROSS

The two faces and halos of the figures on the right-hand side of the group are still discernible.

The farthest to the right is the face of a dark-haired young man with a short beard and close-cropped hair. He is holding rounded vessel. In iconography, objects held by the saints depicted are meaningful. Saints who were doctors or healers would be shown carrying a vessel for medicines or a box for medical instruments. This saint is identifiable as a doctor or healer.

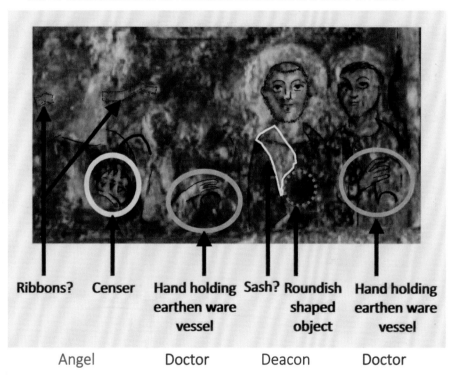

Ribbons?	Censer	Hand holding earthen ware vessel	Sash?	Roundish shaped object	Hand holding earthen ware vessel
Angel		Doctor		Deacon	Doctor

The adjacent figure has a more definite, but still short, beard. He has short, tonsured, hair. Tonsured hair indicates that the saint was a deacon. It is not possible to discern what exactly this saint is holding. However, the discernible dark circular shape could be the remains of the painting of a censer or of a church building. In early Byzantine icons a symbolic church was often portrayed in the shape of a censer, and some censers themselves were made in the shape of churches. Sometimes the dome alone would represent a church building.

A saint holding a church building will be a saint who was particularly important in building up the Church itself. St Peter or Saint Paul might be shown holding a church building, but neither would be tonsured.

Remnants of a white band over his right shoulder might have been a sash; a deacon's stole or 'orarion', another indication of deaconship.

The second saint in from the right can thus be identified as a deacon, and possibly a deacon noted for his role in building up the church.

The third figure in from the right is even less clear. However, it is possible to see that he also is holding a rounded vessel similar to that being held by the figure on the extreme right; a jar associated with a medicinal function. Here we probably have another doctor.

A slightly larger figure, fourth in from the right, is holding a censer. This is very clear. The censer identifies him as an angel or as a deacon. There is no trace of a stole, which would indicate that this saint is a deacon. The possibility of his being an angel is enhanced by the ribbon like shapes which can be seen, though not clearly, to each side of his head. Also, one can see an upward curved line behind his left shoulder which could be the top of an angel's wing. Thus, this figure is extremely likely to be an angel.

From the visual clues we have and a knowledge of the symbolism used in iconography, we can identify the four saints partially visible as: from right to left; a Doctor, a Deacon, a Doctor and an Angel.

WHO ARE THE SAINTS AT THE FOOT OF THE CROSS?

SAINTS COSMAS and DAMIEN

Saints Cosmas and Damien were twin brothers; early Christian martyrs who were doctors. They are almost always shown together in icons. Icons of these saints depict St Cosmas as having short dark hair and a short beard.

The head of the 'doctor 'saint to the extreme right has a short, dark, hair and a beard. The church in which the San Damiano Cross hangs is dedicated to St Damien. It would therefore have been appropriate to depict St Damien in a central position in the panel. It would be a sound deduction to identify the central saint (third in from the right) as St Damien and the saint at the extreme right as his brother, St Cosmas.

The spirituality of these brother saints was wonderfully in tune with the spirituality St Francis was to grow towards. They treated everyone as brothers and sisters in Christ, taking no payment for their services as doctors. They became known as *Anargyroi* in Greek, which translates as 'the penniless ones'; names resonating with St Francis' own title of '*Poverello*', 'the poor one'.

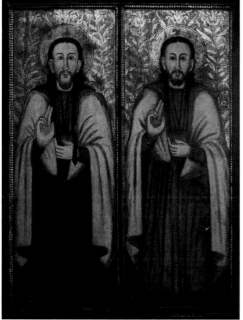

Saints Cosmas and Damien were Syrian. The Syrian saints were venerated throughout the Christian world, but would have been particularly close to the hearts of the Syrian monks in Spoleto.

According to tradition, the holy brothers treated all in both body, as doctors, and soul, as evangelists of The Word. They lived out the gospel, giving freely to the poor and sharing the knowledge of God's love.

Their martyrdom was heroic and awful to contemplate.

Saints Cosmas and Damien, 17th cent icon, Przykuta, Historic Museum, Sanok, Poland.

Their mother and three younger brothers were martyred with them. During the persecution of Christians by Diocletian, they were tortured cruelly in many ways, including being hung on crosses, before being beheaded. Their holy mother witnessed the torture and death of her children, alongside of whom she was martyred.

Their martyrdom resonates with the mother and her seven sons (2 M 7) who were tortured and killed for their obedience to the law of God. Though, in contrast with the Old Testament saints, Comas and Damien forgave their torturers as they committed their souls to God.

At the foot of the cross of Jesus, another mother witnessed the cruel death of her son.

Saints Cosmas and Damien are the patron saints of Doctors. They were buried in Cyrus, in Syria, and a basilica was built over their tombs. It has been in the care of the Franciscan order since 1503. I do not know how it has fared in recent times.

SAINT STEPHEN

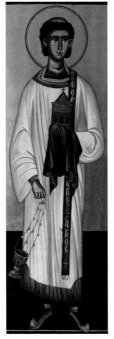

Icon of St Stephen. He holds a hanging censer in his right hand and a church building in his left hand. He wears a deacon's stole (orarion) and his hair is tonsured.

Between the saints I believe to be Cosmas and Damien, is the deacon saint who is very likely to be Saint Stephen.

Icons of St Stephen, the first martyr of Christianity, show him as a young man with short dark tonsured hair, carrying a censer and wearing a deacon's stole or robes. The second saint in from the right is a match for St Stephen.

St Stephen was one of the Greek speaking Jews to be selected by the disciples to ensure that Greek speaking widows were given a fair share of alms to the poor. Again, we have a saint committed to the welfare of the most needy. St Stephen is renowned for his speech to the Sanhedrin, before he was stoned to death. His story is told in The Acts of the Apostles. (6: 8-13; 7:1-60.)

In iconography nothing is random. The San Damiano cross is an icon of the crucifixion. Everything portrayed relates to this salvic event. Saint Stephen's long speech summarises the history of the Chosen People and their relationship with God. It ends with his reference to the crucifixion:

'Was there a prophet whom your ancestors did not persecute? They killed those who announced the coming of the Just One whom you have now betrayed and murdered.'

In accordance with the teaching and example of Jesus, Stephen forgave his persecutors. *'As they were stoning him, Stephen prayed saying: "Lord Jesus receive my spirit." Then he knelt down and said in a loud voice: "Lord, do not hold this sin against them." And when he had said this, he died.'*

It is significant that there is a medieval church in Assisi dedicated to him.

The name Stephen is from the Greek Στέφανος, which means *'crown'*. A crown is used in iconography as a symbol of martyrdom.

THE ANGEL

The evidence, as previously explained, indicates that this figure is an angel, and, in this central position in the panel, would have been an Archangel.

St Michael is the angel saint who was portrayed most often. A great warrior of God, he was one of the patron saints of Umbria.

St Gabriel is the angel most closely linked to our redemption, having been God's chosen messenger to the Virgin Mary. As Mary accepted God's plan, the Lord became incarnate. The incarnation was the beginning of the life of Jesus on earth which was to Come to a climax on Calvary.

The angel portrayed is, in my opinion, more likely to be St Gabriel. The central theme of an icon will always be enhanced, and not ignored, in peripheral content.

'SCHOLARS SAY'

I have read many descriptions of the cross which refer to 'scholars' saying that the saints at the foot of the cross include St Peter, St Paul and St Rufino .

In the language of iconography, saints are easily recognisable. Saint Peter is always shown as having short curly grey hair and a thick, short, curly beard. He would not be represented as a deacon or as a doctor, holding either a censer or an earthen vessel. Saint Paul is shown as having thin dark hair, receding in a wide band centrally from the front within which is a little tuft of hair.

His beard is longish, dark and thin, often shown as a number of fine ringlets rather than as full beard. Saints Peter and Paul are likely to be holding

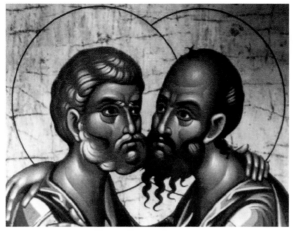

the Word of God, as either a book or scroll. St Peter may be shown holding keys. Their right hands are usually shown as blessing us. Sometimes they might be shown holding the martyr's cross. They would never be shown carrying rounded jars. Neither of the two saints, whose features are discernible, resembles the established characteristics of either Saint Peter or Saint Paul. One prototype icon shows the two saints embracing.

Saint Rufino, having been a bishop, would have been portrayed wearing the formal robes of a bishop. He is not one of saints discernible.

There are no visible clues as to the identity of the two remaining saints. However, we know that in keeping with the 'rules' of iconography, they will have been saints who support the theme of the icon; the Crucifixion.

Given his unique relationship to Jesus, his role in His mission, and his great popularity in the Orthodox Church, I would consider St John the Baptist a saint who might very well have been one of the saints portrayed.

Following the logic of the icon, St Simeon would have been an appropriate saint for the iconographer to have chosen as the final saint. St Simeon recognised the baby Jesus as our Saviour and prophesied His mother's suffering. His words link him to the crucifixion. A New Testament saint, he lived in Jesus' lifetime, as did St John the Baptist.

THE ORIGINAL CROSS

It is now apparent that the original cross had a panel portraying six full length figures of saints at its base and that the entire cross was consistently framed. The illustration on pg. 55 is indicative of how the original cross would have looked.

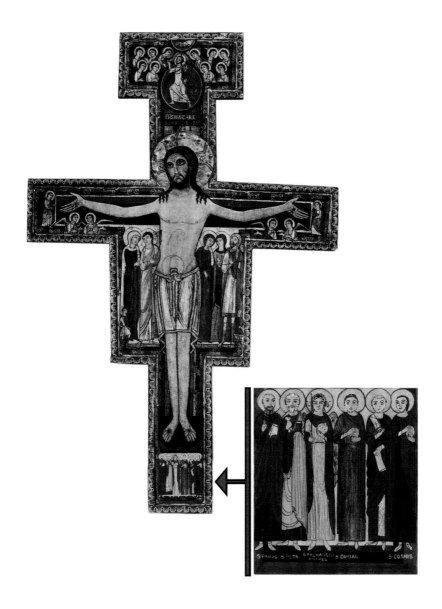

The six 'missing' saints shown include the discernible remnants of the original saints.

The two saints completely lost on the left have been replaced as Saints Peter and Paul. I have included Saints Peter and Paul in the indicative reconstruction of the cross, not because I believe that those saints would have been portrayed, but to show how easy it would be to recognise them, had they been any of the saints partially visible.

The two centre saints have been reconstructed as an Archangel and St Damien. St Stephen, is between St Damien adjacent to the left, and St Cosmas on the extreme right.

I am indebted to my friend, Kieran Brogan, for his assistance in providing this image. Although I have a good technical drawing programme, I have no skills with photo manipulation. Kieran was so patient, adjusting colour and size until we got the inset right!

MODERN SCIENCE

This study of The San Damiano Cross is based on an understanding of iconography and of what we can see in the cross today.

The recently published study of the San Damiano Cross, *Franceso e la Croce di S. Damiano* by Milvia Bollati, published by Edizioni Biblioteca Francescana, is a book of exceptional quality and it includes a detailed scientific study of the cross. Illustrations no 10 and no 74 show the cross extending down, confirming exactly, in terms of dimensions, the conclusion I have presented above. This is an amazing and wonderful confluence of two completely different types of investigation. My own is rooted in a knowledge of the ancient and sacred art of iconography and the visual imagery of the front of the cross.

Milvia Bollatti's investigations used the most modern equipment and benefitted from having the cross in laboratory conditions. Two totally different methods, and yet the findings, in terms of the length of the original cross, coincide perfectly.

Milvia Bollatti's work is far more extensive and I would in no way compare my study to her comprehensive and thoroughly researched investigation into every aspect of the cross. I am indebted to her also for the historic images of the cross included in her book. These will be of great assistance to me in preparing drawings for a reconstruction of the San Damiano Cross as a new icon.

GEOMETRY

Having established the probable original size of the icon and identified how it might have looked, a deeper look at the geometry of the original icon may be of interest to some.

The illustration below shows just a tiny sample of the disciplined geometry underpinning the design of the cross, attesting to the coherence and sophistication of the proportions and dimensioning found in iconography.

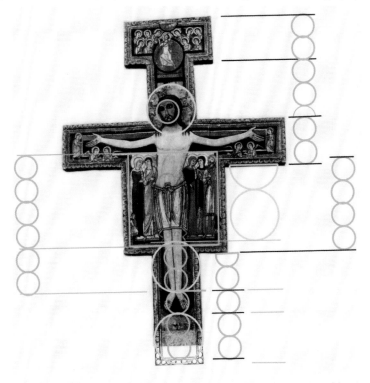

D1   Circles having a diameter of 3n. 3n is the length of the face of Jesus.

D2   Circles having a diameter of 6.5n. 6.5n is the height of Jesus' halo.

Sacred geometry underlies every aspect of the icon. Every line is based on disciplined geometric relationships. Arcs, tangents, dimensions: all are based on key diameters expressed in units of 'n'. ('n'= the length of Jesus' nose.)

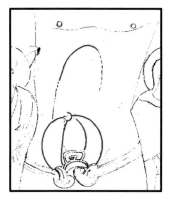

I tried a little experiment. I chose just five lines; fine, clear lines on the icon defining Jesus' abdomen and chest. I found that these lines were constructed from various arcs of circles, all of which had diameters which were multiples of 'n'. I was able to produce eleven illustrations showing how these arcs related to the drawing of the saints adjacent. I have chosen two as examples.

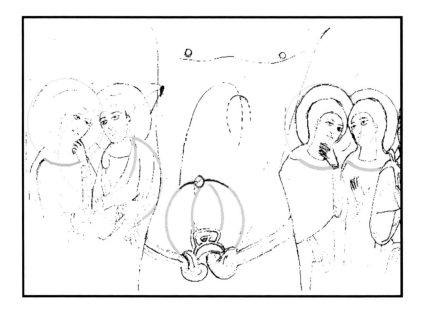

The illustration above reflects just a hint of the beauty of the line drawing, based as it is on a geometric discipline of interweaving arcs. This illustration shows arcs of diameter 2.5n in turquoise. Note particularly the close relationship between the drawing of Jesus' abdomen, the garment of St John, (his body) and the head and halo of the Mother of God.

The 'Arc of Heaven' at the top of the cross also has an arc of 2.5n.

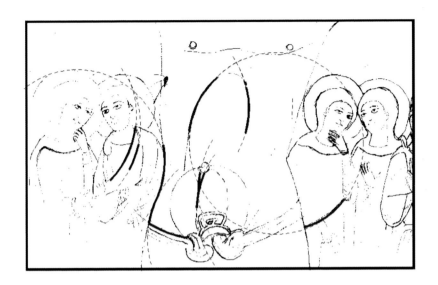

This illustration of the same area of the image shows arcs and construction circles having a diameter of 5.5n. Again, this shows so well the beautiful closeness between St John and Jesus and The Mother of God.

Conformity to geometric relationships is linked to the theology of harmony and obedience. A study of any aspect of creation will show God's love of the harmony and functionality found in mathematical relationships. The seed head of a sunflower is formed as, one by one, embryonic seeds form in the centre of the developing seed head, and then move out at an angle of 137.5.' The resulting seed head is packed with seeds, set in interweaving patterns of swirls. It is a work of art, perfectly efficient in its function. Conformity to God's will brings order. Order in iconography is indicative of obedience to His Holy will.

The sacred geometry in the icon is based on circles, which symbolise the eternal nature of God. The unit of measurement is derived from the Holy Face.

There is nothing in the icon which does not conform to geometric relationships, weaving the various components into a seamless whole. It is rich in balance and harmony, the source of which is not discerned, only the result.

The San Damiano Cross exhibits many more subtle refinements in order to ensure a harmonious and visually balanced design; a design which is also true to the language of iconography and its strict adherence to theological truth. To give one example: the panel showing the witnesses to the crucifixion is slightly longer on the left side than it is on the right. This allows the two most important witnesses to be painted bigger than the saints on the right.

DRAWING STYLE

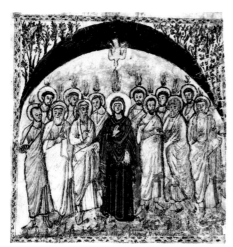

The icon has Coptic origins. It was most likely to have been painted by Syrian monks who had settled in Spoleto to evade persecution. It is essentially a 'line' drawing not dissimilar to that found in the illustrations in the Rabbula Gospels (AD 586) which display *'a strong Hellenistic heritage within a specific Syrian tradition'[4]*. The lines are not loose or random. They are knitted together on a web of related arcs. This discipline is not obvious to the eye, but it is there, bringing harmony and unity to the whole. The colour palette is restricted but harmoniously balanced throughout. Other early medieval crosses, such as Alberto Sotio's icon in the Duomo in Spoleto, show strong similarities to the San Damiano cross. The San Damiano Cross is closest to its Byzantine roots in having retained the 'frame' element of classic iconography and in not being signed. Monks who painted icons were not seeking personal acknowledgement of their artistry. In their humility these iconographers generally did not sign their work. As the figures in Alberto Sotio's crucifixion are more sculpted, and the face and hair of Jesus more modelled, it is likely to have been painted at a later date than The San Damiano Cross. The face and hair of Jesus seen on one early medieval cross. (Croce Dipinta, della chiesa di S. Paulo all'Orta in Pisa) are very similar to the face and hair of Jesus on the San Damiano Cross. This work dates from the first quarter of the twelfth century suggesting a similar date for The San Damiano Cross.

---

[4] Weitzmann Kurt, *Late Antique and Early Christian Book Illumination,* N.Y. George Brazilier, Inc.

PAINTING TECHNIQUE.

The icon was painted using egg tempera on a gessoed ground. A linen, or similar fabric, would have been glued to the wood of the cross and gesso applied on top.

Gesso is a mixture of powdered white chalk or marble and a natural (rabbit skin) glue. It is painted on in layers whilst warm and fluid. When hard, it is sanded and polished until it has the texture of polished bone. It is brilliant white. The main lines of the design would have been cut into the gesso.

Finely beaten gold was used to gild the backdrops on the panels portraying the angels and saints. A heavier gold, secured with studs, was used for the border and for Jesus' halo.

Egg tempera uses pigments, finely ground, applied in thin layers using a solution of egg yolk laced with vinegar. The iconographer starts with base colours; the darkest tone in any one area. 'Lights' are then added, in controlled geometric shapes. The whole process reflects spiritual dimensions. The wood; the wood of the cross, the white linen cloth; the shroud, the gold: the uncreated light of God, the geometric shapes: the spiritual and non-material essence of the icon, the working from dark to light: the spiritual movement from darkness into 'The Light'.

PRAYING WITH ICONS

Icons are visual theology. Their role is to lead the viewer into the spiritual. There is no need for set prayers. Let the icon speak to your heart and respond, as Francis did, with prayer of the heart.

Like any relationship, the communion between viewer and icon grows with time in each other's company.

The icon is a doorway into all things of God. There is no limit to the depth of response it can engender.

Light candles in front of your icon; touch it, kiss it with reverential love. The veneration given to the icon is veneration of the prototype, of the saint depicted. Open your heart to listen to the icon and pray before it as the Holy Spirit inspires.

In the Orthodox Church, icons are integral to liturgy and worship. There are many books available to guide you in appreciating and praying with icons.

This booklet can only hope to nudge open a door of awareness, if it has not been opened already.

For obvious and valid reasons, the original San Damiano Cross is 'out of reach' for close personal veneration.

There is a copy in the little chapel attached to the house of St Francis' parents. It is hung low enough to be able to be near it when praying with it.

When you buy your own copy, let it be of a size you can have close to you. Avoid crosses with gaudy frames which detract seriously from the integrity of the icon's perfectly balanced design.

In 'Lectio Divina' the Holy Spirit may inspire some very personal insights for your contemplation. So also, in contemplating this exceptionally beautiful and masterful icon, the Holy Spirit will gift treasures particular to you.

You have the prayers of a saint when, in the shoes of St Francis, you open your heart before it. The Syrian monk who painted it, fasting and praying as he worked, prayed for every person who would venerate it throughout the ages.

The language and symbolism found in classic Byzantine icons was gradually lost in the West as 'realism' in religious art gained favour. However, the San Damiano Cross is a perfect example of a perfect icon. It is a doorway, a window to the spiritual realm of the Divine Godhead. Contemplation of this icon, soundly based as it is on biblical truths, can only bring you closer into the mystery of God and our redemption through the crucifixion of our Loving Lord Jesus.

When Paula asked me to give a talk about an icon I knew nothing about, I had no realisation of the journey into love which I was setting out on.

It is my hope that this presentation on the cross will give you, as it did me, a greater appreciation of this unique and holy icon and assist you in your prayer and meditation as you spend time with your crucified Lord.

FURTHER READING

St Francis:

Carmody, M. *The Franciscan Story: St Francis of Assisi and his influence since the Thirteenth Century,* London, Athena Press, 2008.

Vauchez, A. *Francis of Assisi; The Life and Afterlife of a Medieval Saint,* Yale, Cusato M. (trans) University Press, 2012, originally published in French as *Francois d'Assisi: Entre Histoire et Memoire,* Librairie Artheme Fayard, 2009.

Englebert, O. *Saint Francis of Assisi,* E Hutton (trans.) London, Burns and Oates, 1950.

Galli, M. *Francis of Assisi and his World,* Downers Grove, IL, InterVarsity Press, 2002.

Bodo O.F.M., M. *Francis: The Journey and the Dream,* Cincinnati, OH, St. Anthony Messenger Press, 2012.

Bodo O.F.M., M . *Enter Assisi: An Invitation to Franciscan Spirituality,* Cincinnati, OH, Franciscan Media Press, 2015.

Iconography:

Article recommended by Claus Scheifele OFM: **Moutsoulas, Elias D.** *Theology of the Icon, www.myriobiblos.gr/texts*

Aidan Hart gives a list of sound references on his website; aidanharticons.com go to: Resources/Icon Related Books/Theology and History of the Icon.

I would add this book, written as a basic introduction to icons:

Martin, L. *Sacred Doorways-A Beginner's Guide to Icons,* Brewster, Massachusetts, Paraclete Press, 2002.

and three of my own favourite references:

Cavarnos, C. *Guide to Byzantine Iconography, Volumes One and Two,* Massachusetts, USA, Institute for Byzantine and Modern Greek Studies, 2001.

Terzopoulis, Rev Dr Constantine, (trans.) *What Do You Know About Icons,* Holy Monastery of Saint John the Baptist Kareas, Attiki, Greece, Etoimasia Publications, 2001.

Tradigo, A. (translated by; Sartarelli, S.), *Icons and Saints of the Eastern Orthodox Church,* Los Angelos, USA, J.Paul Getty Museum, 2006

The San Damiano Cross:

Bollati, M. *Francesco e la croce di S. Damiano,* Milano, Italy, Edizioni Biblioteca Francescana, 2016. (A comprehensive and detailed study of the physical features of the San Damiano Cross with references to similar art works. {in Italian})

The following present deep spiritual insights and make helpful links to biblical texts. Some of their interpretations of the visual imagery of the San Damiano Cross are, in my opinion, open to discussion.

Picard OFM Cap, M. *The Icon of the Christ of San Damiano,* Assisi, Italy, Casa Editrice Francescana, 2000.

Baldyga, S. *The San Damiano Cross,* Assisi, Italy, Porziuncola, 2001.

Guinan OFM, M. *The Franciscan Vision and the Gospel of St John,* St Bonaventure, NY, USA Franciscan Institute Press, 2006.

IMAGES

The many images of The San Damiano Cross in this booklet are derived from the image obtained from Adobe Stock; © Kreuz; San Damiano; Santa Chiara, Assis/stockadobe.com., through www.kieranbroganphotography.com (Pg 12.)

Pg 7: San Damiano, **Attribution**: Superchilum (CC BY-SA 3.0) Wikimedia Creative Commons

Pg 8: Landscape, **Attribution**: Friedhelm Droge (CC BY-SA Creative Commons BY-SA/3.0)

Pg.10: San Damiano (interior), **Attribution**: Berthold Werner (Public Domain)

Pg 14: Examples of Medieval painted crosses damaged at base: With thanks to Wikimedia Commons: from left to right:
1. Croce Dipinta (Chiesa di Sant' Angeloal Cassero Pinacoteca) Municipal Art Gallery Castiglion, Fiorentino. Anonymous Unknown author (Public Domain)
2. Di Maestro Senese di Inizio Duecento, Crocifisso da S. Chiara. **Attribution:** Combuskin
3. Giovanni da Rimini 14th c, Crucifix. **Attribution**: Sailko (CC BY-SA 3.0) Creative Commons

Pg. 17: Attributions and titles indicated with images on page.

Pg. 21: With thanks to Wikimedia Commons for both images.
Top: Theotokos Hodegetria 16th c **Attribution**: Sinebrychoff Museum, Finnish National Gallery, Public Domain.
Lower: Head of Virgin Mary, Cretan School 17thc. Pushkin Museum. **Attribution**: Иоанн Апакксс (Public Domain).
Amended image with dimensions and grids: Madeleine Stewart

Pg. 36: With thanks to Wikimedia Creative Commons: Travelling Icon of the Crucifixion, Weimer Schlossmuseum, **Attribution**: Dguendel (CC BY 4.0)

Pg. 42: With thanks to Wikimedia Commons for all four images of full crosses. Cropping to focus on bases of crosses et:, Madeleine Stewart.
1, Di Maestro Senese di Inizio Duecento, Crocifisso da S. Chiara. **Attribution:** Combuskin
2. Croce Dipinta (Chiesa di Sant' Angeloal Cassero Pinacoteca) Municipal Art Gallery Castiglion, Fiorentino. Anonymous Unknown author (Public Domain)
3. Francesco di Segna, 1328-39, Sienese School, Paintings in the Museum of Sacred Art of Val d'Arbia, Bounoconvento.**Attribution**: Francesco di Segna, (Public Domain).
4. Gionanni da Rimini, 14th c. Crucifix.**Attribution**: Sailko {CC BY-SA 3.0) Creative Commons

Pg. 51: Saints Cosmas and Damien, 17th c. Historic Museum in Sanok, Poland by Przykuta. **Attribution**: Przykuta, Wikimedia Commons, (Public Domain)

Pg 52: Icon Agios Stephano, Crete, Church of Agios Stephanos, Lasithi Region. **Attribution**: Abaddon 1337 (CC BY 4) Wikmedia Creative Commons, (Public Domain.)

Pg 54: St Peter and St. Paul Kiss, Adobe Stock

Pg. 55: I could not have produced this image without Kieran Brogan's skilled assistance.

Pg. 60: Pentecost, Rabula Gospels, Wiki Commons folio 14v. **Attribution**: Meister des Rabula-Evangeliums, (Public Domain)

All other diagrams and images: Madeleine Stewart